INSIDE YOUR BODY

ALL ABOUT PINK EYE

MEGAN BORGERT-SPANIOL

Consulting Editor, Diane Craig, MA/Reading Specialist

Super Sandcastle

An Imprint of Abdo Publishing
abdopublishing.com

ABDOPUBLISHING.COM

Published by Abdo Publishing, a division of ABDO, PO Box 398166, Minneapolis, Minnesota 55439. Copyright © 2019 by Abdo Consulting Group, Inc. International copyrights reserved in all countries. No part of this book may be reproduced in any form without written permission from the publisher. Super SandCastle™ is a trademark and logo of Abdo Publishing.

Printed in the United States of America, North Mankato, Minnesota
052018
092018

Design and Production: Mighty Media, Inc.
Editor: Jessie Alkire
Cover Photographs: iStockphoto; Shutterstock
Interior Photographs: iStockphoto; Shutterstock

Library of Congress Control Number: 2017961870

Publisher's Cataloging-in-Publication Data

Names: Borgert-Spaniol, Megan, author.
Title: All about pink eye / by Megan Borgert-Spaniol.
Description: Minneapolis, Minnesota : Abdo Publishing, 2019. |
    Series: Inside your body set 2
Identifiers: ISBN 9781532115820 (lib.bdg.) | ISBN 9781532156540
    (ebook)
Subjects: LCSH: Human body--Juvenile literature. | Conjunctivitis--
    Juvenile literature. | Infection in children--Juvenile literature. |
    Bacterial diseases--Juvenile literature. | Communicable diseases-
    Juvenile literature.
Classification: DDC 617.7--dc23

Super SandCastle™ books are created by a team of professional educators, reading specialists, and content developers around five essential components—phonemic awareness, phonics, vocabulary, text comprehension, and fluency—to assist young readers as they develop reading skills and strategies and increase their general knowledge. All books are written, reviewed, and leveled for guided reading, early reading intervention, and Accelerated Reader™ programs for use in shared, guided, and independent reading and writing activities to support a balanced approach to literacy instruction.

CONTENTS

YOUR BODY

You're amazing! So is your body.

Most of the time your body works just fine. It lets you go to school, play with friends, and more. But sometimes you feel sick or part of you hurts.

any kids get pink eye. It can make your eyes red and **itchy**. Most cases of pink eye are not serious. But you should treat pink eye right away. It can spread quickly!

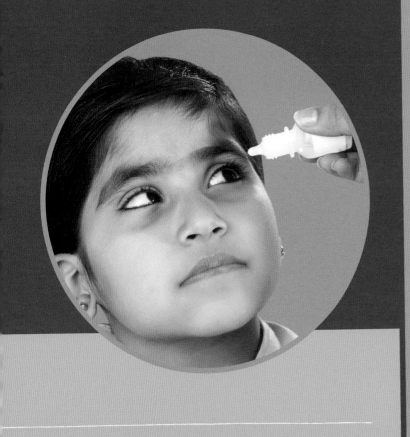

ALL ABOUT PINK EYE

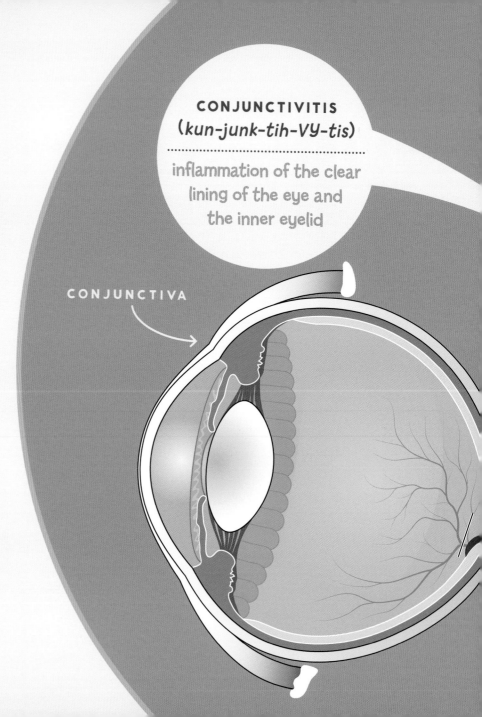

CONJUNCTIVITIS
(kun-junk-tih-VY-tis)
....
inflammation of the clear lining of the eye and the inner eyelid

CONJUNCTIVA

Pink eye is the **inflammation** of one or both eyes. It is also called conjunctivitis. That's because it affects part of the eye called the conjunctiva. This is a clear tissue. It covers the white part of the eyeball. It also lines the inside of the eyelid.

The conjunctiva has tiny blood vessels. **Inflammation** makes the vessels easier to see. This makes the eye look pink or red. That's why the condition is commonly called pink eye!

A VIRUS THAT CAUSES
PINK EYE

INFECTIONS

Most cases of pink eye are **infections** caused by viruses or bacteria.

These are often the same viruses and bacteria that cause other illnesses. You can get pink eye when you're sick with one of these illnesses.

Cold

A cold is an infection of the nose and throat. It is caused by a virus.

Common **symptoms**: stuffy nose, sore throat, coughing

Ear Infection

An ear **infection** happens when tubes in your ear get infected. Liquid builds up and can cause pain.

Common **symptoms**: ear pain, trouble hearing, ear drainage

Sinus Infection

Your sinuses are open spaces in your skull. Liquid can get trapped in these spaces. This can cause an infection.

Common symptoms: fever, runny nose, pain or pressure in the face

Sore Throat

Most sore throats are symptoms of viral infections. But sometimes they are caused by bacterial infections.

Common symptoms: scratchy throat, pain when swallowing, fever

ALLERGIES
AND IRRITANTS

Sometimes pink eye is not caused by an **infection**. **Allergies** and **irritants** can also cause pink eye.

Allergies

Some people have allergies. This means their bodies are extra sensitive to things in their **environment**. Things that cause allergic **reactions** are called allergens.

COMMON ALLERGENS THAT CAUSE PINK EYE

GRASS

POLLEN

ANIMAL HAIR

DUST

Signs of allergic pink eye: **itchy**, watery eyes, sneezing, runny nose

Irritants

Pink eye can be caused by things that get in the eye and **irritate** it. These things are called irritants.

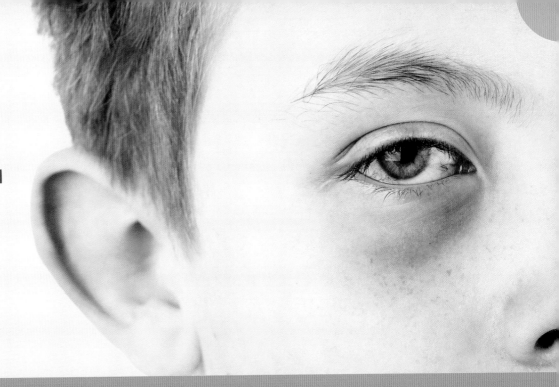

COMMON IRRITANTS THAT CAUSE PINK EYE

AIR POLLUTION

CHLORINE IN POOLS

HOUSEHOLD CLEANERS

SMOKE

Signs of irritant pink eye: watery, red eyes that clear up within about a day

PINK EYE

Pink eye caused by an **infection** is contagious. This means it can easily spread from person to person. Pink eye can spread through coughing and sneezing. It is also passed through contact with liquid from the eyes.

1. A person with pink eye touches his eyes.

2. He touches a friend's hand.

3. His friend touches her own eyes.

How does pink eye spread?

You can also pass pink eye to yourself! If you have it in one eye, you can spread it to the other eye. This happens if you touch your healthy eye after touching your **infected** eye.

No Infection, No Passing

Pink eye caused by **allergies** or **irritants** is not contagious. That's because there are no viruses or bacteria to pass along!

1. A person with pink eye touches his eye.

2. He touches an object such as a ball or door handle.

3. His friend touches the same object and then touches her own eyes.

SIGNS
AND SYMPTOMS

If you have pink eye, you will probably see it! The white part of your eye will turn pink or red. Pink eye usually comes with other **symptoms** too. These symptoms can occur in one or both eyes.

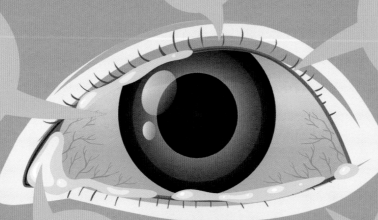

SWOLLEN
EYELID

EYELASHES
STUCK
TOGETHER
AFTER SLEEP

PINK OR
RED EYE

ITCHY
EYE

WATERY OR
PUS-LIKE
LIQUID COMING
FROM EYE

FEELING LIKE
SAND IS IN
YOUR EYE

Virus or Bacteria?

The liquid from your eyes may be watery. It can also be **pus**-like. It is usually watery if your **infection** is caused by a virus. If the liquid is pus-like, your infection is likely bacterial.

Bacterial pink eye is contagious as soon as your **symptoms** appear. Viral pink eye can spread to others before symptoms appear. Both kinds of pink eye are contagious until symptoms pass.

GOING TO THE
DOCTOR

It can be hard to know which kind of pink eye you have. If you notice signs of pink eye, it's important to see a doctor right away. This reduces the risk of getting other serious illnesses. Your doctor will find out the cause of your pink eye.

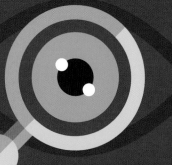

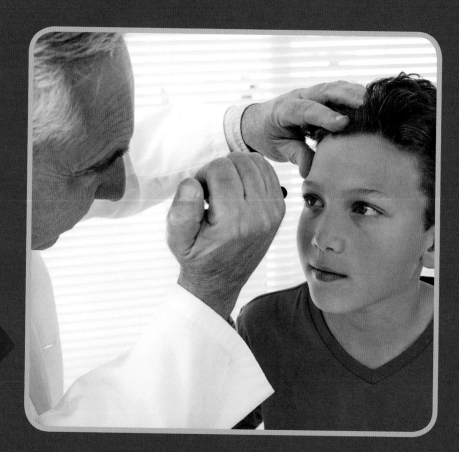

There are several ways your doctor might learn the cause of your **symptoms**.

- Ask you about your symptoms

- Examine your eyes

- Examine your ears for signs of an ear **infection**

- Take a sample of the liquid draining from your eyes and send it to a lab for testing

Once your doctor knows the cause of your symptoms, she can help you treat them!

TREATMENT

Your doctor may **prescribe** medicine to treat your **symptoms**. But this depends on the cause of your pink eye.

Cause	Treatment
BACTERIAL INFECTION	DOCTOR MAY PRESCRIBE ANTIBIOTIC EYE DROPS OR OINTMENT
VIRAL INFECTION	USUALLY GOES AWAY WITHOUT MEDICINE
ALLERGIES	DOCTOR MAY PRESCRIBE ALLERGY EYE DROPS OR OTHER ALLERGY MEDICINES
IRRITANT	USUALLY GOES AWAY WITHOUT MEDICINE

Home Remedies

You can also do things to relieve your pink eye **symptoms** at home.

• Gently clean your eye with a cotton ball dipped in warm water.

• If your eyelashes are stuck together after sleep, keep your eye closed. Place a warm cloth over the eye to loosen the crust.

• Take pain relievers or use eye drops to relieve discomfort.

• If you wear contact lenses, stop wearing them until your symptoms go away. Ask your doctor if you should throw away **infected** lenses.

RED ALERT!

Your eyes should feel better soon. Depending on the cause of your pink eye, **symptoms** should get better in two to seven days.

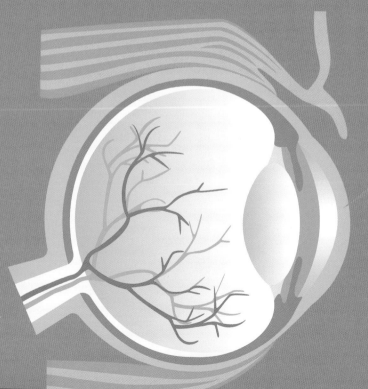

CORNEA
(KORN-ee-ah)

·······················

the clear part of the eyeball that focuses light passing into the eye

Call your doctor if your pink eye is not going away. This could mean you have another illness too. These may include an ear **infection**, sinus infection, or **inflammation** of the cornea.

Watch out for signs that your pink eye needs medical attention.

- Increased eye redness

- Increased swelling of eyelids

- Severe eye pain

- Blurry vision

- Sensitivity to light

- Ear pain

- Fever

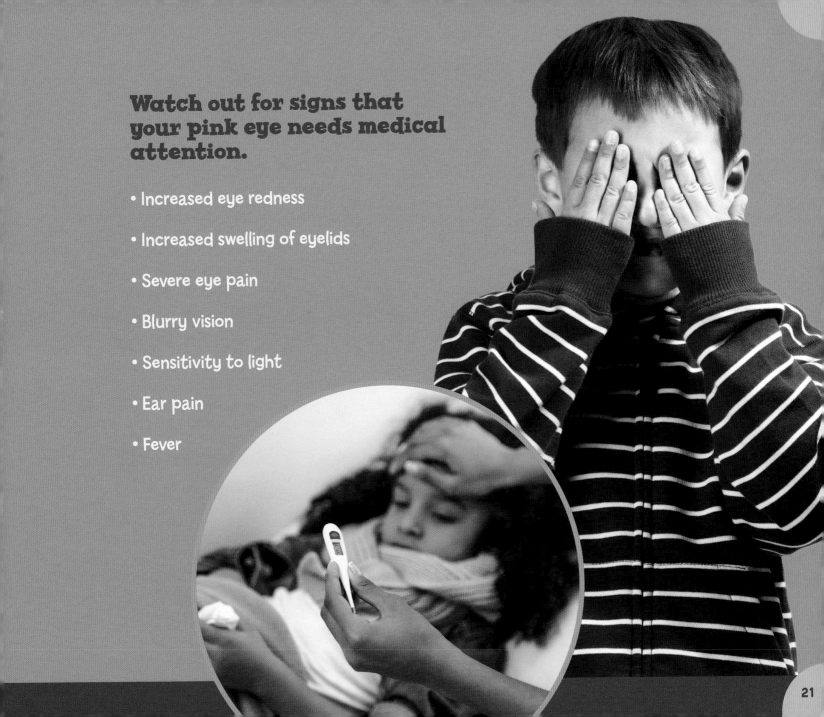

PREVENTION

Do **allergies** or **irritants** give you pink eye? Try to avoid things that cause allergic **reactions** or pain.

CLOSE WINDOWS AND DOORS WHEN POLLEN IS HEAVY OUTSIDE.

DUST AND VACUUM YOUR HOME OFTEN.

AVOID HOUSEHOLD CLEANERS AND OTHER CHEMICALS.

There are also ways you can prevent the spread of pink eye **infections**.

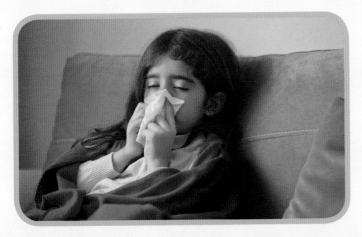

IF YOU HAVE PINK EYE, STAY HOME FROM SCHOOL UNTIL LIQUID NO LONGER DRAINS FROM YOUR EYES.

DON'T SHARE WASHCLOTHS, TOWELS, OR PILLOWCASES.

AVOID TOUCHING YOUR EYES WITH YOUR HANDS.

WASH YOUR HANDS WITH WARM WATER AND SOAP, ESPECIALLY AFTER TOUCHING YOUR EYES!

ALLERGY – a sickness caused by touching, breathing, or eating certain things. Something related to an allergy is called allergic.

ENVIRONMENT – surroundings.

INFECT – to cause sickness by spreading bacteria or other germs. Such a sickness is an infection.

INFLAMMATION – the body's response to injury or irritation. It can cause swelling, redness, and pain.

IRRITATE – to make sore or painful. Something that causes this is an irritant.

ITCHY – feeling irritated or bothersome.

PRESCRIBE – to order the use of a medicine or treatment.

PUS – a thick, yellowish substance the body produces when it has an infection.

REACTION – a response to a stimulus.

SYMPTOM – a noticeable change in the normal working of the body.

GLOSSARY